Exploring the Mass

Bishop Vincent Nichols

Student's Book

CATHOLIC TRUTH SOCIETY

PUBLISHERS TO THE HOLY SEE

Nihil Obstat:
Father Anton Cowan (Censor)
Imprimatur:
Rt. Rev. Patrick O'Donoghue, V.G. Bishop in West London
Westminster, 6th May 1999

The Nihil Obstat and Imprimatur are a declaration that a book or pamphlet is considered to be free from doctrinal or moral error. It is not implied that those who have granted the Nihil Obstat and Imprimatur agree with the contents, opinions or statements expressed.

Design, compilation and format copyright © 1999 The Incorporated Catholic Truth Society.
Text copyright © Marcellina Cooney. Published 1999 by the Incorporated Catholic Truth Society,
40-46 Harleyford Road, London SE11 5AY
Telephone: (0207) 640 0042 Fax: (0207) 640 0046

ISBN: 186082 067 0

Designed and Produced by: The Catholic Truth Society/Stephen Campbell.

Illustrations: © Jill Hunt/The Beehive Illustration Agency, unless stated below.

Photography: © Carlos Reyes-Manzo/Andes Press Agency, unless stated below.

Front Cover image: *Abraham and the Three Angels*, icon (tempera on panel), from Macedonia, c.1700, Greek School (18th century) Richardson and Kailas Icons, London/Bridgeman Art Library.

The publisher would also like to thank the the following contributors: *Page 17*, The Prodigal's Return by John Byam Liston Shaw (1872-1919) Russell-Cotes Art Gallery and Museum/Bridgeman Art Library; *page 20,* image courtesy of PhotoDisc Europe Ltd; *page 28,* © Stephen Campbell 'Loaves & Fishes'; *page 35* Bishop Nichols © Purple Media; *page 40* The Last Supper, 1865 (pencil on paper) by Sir Edward Burne-Jones (1833-98) Birmingham Museums and Art Gallery/Bridgeman Art Library; *page 41* The Last Supper by Leonardo da Vinci (1452-1519) Santa Maria della Grazie, Milan/Bridgeman Art Library; *page 42* Bishop Nichols © Purple Media; *page 50* © Gideon Mendel, with many thanks to CAFOD; *page 59* © William Carson; All Biblical quotations from *The Jerusalem Bible (DLT)* and from *The Good News Bible (Bible Society).*

Also available as part of this resource:
1. Exploring the Mass, Teacher's Resource Book: ISBN 186082 066 2 (Order Ref. Ed 02)

2. Exploring the Mass, Video (40 Minutes): (Order Ref. Ed 03)

3. Thinking Simply about the Mass: ISBN 186082 284 3 (Order Ref. Do 728)

Contents

Introduction

Welcome to 'Exploring the Mass'.

In these lessons you will be studying all about the Mass. There is a video which goes with the lessons contained in this book. I hope you enjoy the study and learn a great deal.

Going to Mass, joining the prayer of the Mass, is the most important thing that Catholics do. It is so important that in times of persecution people have given up all they owned, all their belongings and even their very lives, in order to go to Mass. Others risked their lives by giving shelter to the priest who had come to celebrate Mass with them.

In these lessons you will learn about the Mass and all that it contains. This will help you to understand what happens during the Mass and why it is so precious and unique. I realise that you will have been to Mass many times. But it is such a rich mystery that there is always more to learn about it.

In these lessons you will also have the opportunity to think about what the Mass means to you and how you can take part in it more fully. When people say that they are bored during Mass, I think that it is partly due to the fact that they do not know how to join in the Mass in their hearts and in their minds. I hope these lessons will help you to learn how to do so. Step by step you will come to treasure the Mass yourselves.

Everyone who prepared these materials and the video have enjoyed doing so. I thank them all, especially the late Cardinal Hume, the teachers and RE Adviser in North and East London, and the teachers and pupils of Blessed Thomas Holford High School. I hope that you enjoy your study. There is so much to learn and to appreciate in our faith today.

✠ Vincent Nichols

✠ **Bishop Vincent Nichols**
May 1999

Section 1. Overview
of the
Mass

In this section you will

- reflect on reasons for going to Mass;

- have some understanding of an overview of the Mass;

- understand the signs and symbols used in the Mass;

- know the order of the Mass.

The Mass

Why go to Mass?

We go to Mass
- To worship God our Father;
- To pray with the Catholic Community.

In the Mass, it is Jesus who prays with us and in us. He is the beloved Son of the Father. He said: 'The Father and I are one'.

We need to turn to God and to pray to him in order to keep ourselves right. We have a duty to go to Mass. It is not something that comes from outside of us. It comes from within us, it is in our hearts. We owe it to ourselves to pray and the Mass is the finest prayer.

The important day for going to Mass is Sunday. It is the first day of the week, the day on which Jesus rose from the dead.

Over to You

What do you think are good reasons for going to Mass?

Here are some pupils' reasons for going to Mass

- To pray;
- Because my Mum makes me;
- To praise and thank God;
- I go because I have to;
- It is an opportunity to meet other people;
- To receive Jesus in Holy Communion;
- To ask for forgiveness for our sins;
- To listen to the Lord's message and teaching;
- To make present Jesus' death on the Cross;
- To find support;
- To meet God, who is Father and friend;
- It just makes me feel peaceful;
- It is an opportunity to sing with others;
- I can hand over all my worries to the Lord.

Overview of the Mass

Over to You

1. Draw a circle and divide it into six parts. For each part of your circle, draw an arrow and six boxes as shown below. Put into each box a particular heading as shown.

   Fill in your boxes by choosing the right sentence from the list below.

   - We receive Jesus.
   - We listen to God speaking to us.
   - We tell God we are sorry for the times we have hurt God and each other.
   - The bread and wine become the body and blood of Jesus.
   - The gifts of bread and wine, and of other offerings, are brought up to the altar.

2. One of the boxes you have drawn needs a heading. What do you think it should be? Fill it in and write a statement to explain it.

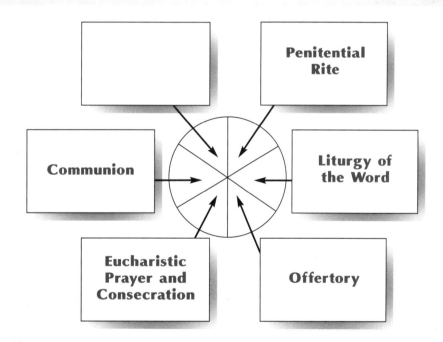

Extension Work

3. Look back to the reasons pupils gave for going to Mass. Try to place these reasons into those boxes that seem best fitted. Some reasons may fit into more than one box.

Signs & Symbols in the Mass

Task

The boxes below explain the signs and symbols used in the Mass.

In your exercise book make a list of the signs and symbols from the Word and Picture Bank and put the right the explanation beside it.

.... The cup for the wine

.... Table for sacrifice

.... Used to give light, now a symbol of light in the darkness

.... Clothes to show the priest takes on a new identity of Jesus

.... Sign of unity, a greeting to other members of the family/church

.... A sacrifice of love, which showed us the extraordinary love God has for us

.... Is changed into the body of Jesus Christ

.... Saying in whose name we gather

.... Is changed into the blood of Jesus

Word and Picture Bank

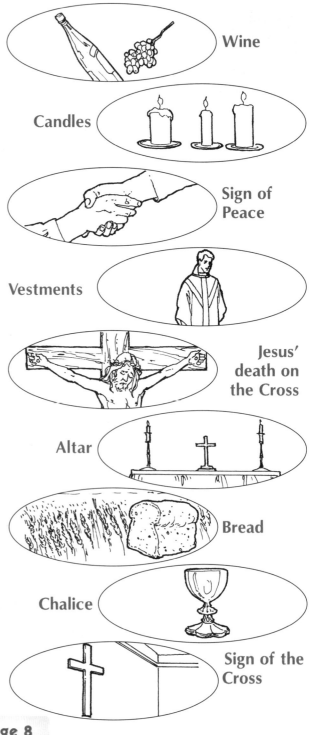

Wine

Candles

Sign of Peace

Vestments

Jesus' death on the Cross

Altar

Bread

Chalice

Sign of the Cross

The Order of the Mass

Over to You

Below is shown the order of the Mass. On the right are some explanations, but not in any particular order. Can you place each part of the Mass with the description that fits best? (Write out the number with the letter beside it).

For example, if you think 'Sign of the Cross' fits with 'Saying in whose name we gather', the answer would be 1(c).

1. **Sign of the Cross**

2. **Penitential Rite**

3. **Gloria**

4. **Readings**

5. **Responsorial Psalm**

6. **Gospel**

7. **Homily**

8. **Creed**

9. **Offertory**

10. **Preparation of the Gifts**

11. **Eucharistic Prayer**

12. **Communion**

13. **Blessing & Dismissal**

(a) A story in one of the Gospels about the life and teaching of Jesus.

(b) A proclamation which says what Catholics believe.

(c) Saying in whose name we gather.

(d) We respond to God in the words of the Bible using prayer-songs from the Old Testament.

(e) We ask forgiveness and healing for any sin that separates us from each other and from God.

(f) We receive Jesus as spiritual food.

(g) God's blessing is called down upon us and we are sent forth to serve the Lord.

(h) The bread and wine are brought to the altar.

(i) Passages from either the Old or New Testament, but not one of the Gospels.

(j) We rejoice in the goodness of God.

(k) Our gifts are presented at the altar.

(l) A prayer, praising God, calling down the Holy Spirit, retelling the Last Supper story, and with the words of Jesus changing the bread into his body and the wine into his blood.

(m) The priest talks to us about the readings.

Our Deepest Desire is for God

Extension Work (1)

"You have made us for yourself, O Lord and our hearts are restless, until they find rest in You" (St. Augustine)

If we look closely at ourselves we will discover that as soon as we get what we want, we want something else and then something else. We can go chasing after one thing, then another, and yet desire something else. As we grow up we realise that there is always a longing and a need within us. St. Augustine explains this very well when he said that God has made us for himself and that the very deepest desire, deep down within us is for God. It is in making time for God in our lives that we will experience a deep inner peace:

"My own peace I give you, a peace the world cannot give, this is my gift to you." (John 14:27)

We need to recognise God and to turn to God. We need to turn to God in prayer, to ask for his guidance in order to keep ourselves right. In this sense we have a duty to pray, because if we don't we will lose our sense of who we are, who we are to be, what we are to do, of what is right and wrong. The duty to pray is not something that comes from outside of us. It is written within our hearts. We owe it to ourselves to pray. To go to Mass is the very greatest prayer that we can participate in. We have a duty to God who made us, who gives us life. That duty is to worship Him. This duty is fulfilled by going to Mass. To deliberately choose not to do so is to offend God. It is a sin for which I must seek forgiveness.

The important day for going to Mass is Sunday. It is the first day of the week, the Lord's Day. It is the day on which Jesus rose from the dead. Sunday is the day of new life. On this day the Church praises God for all his gifts. The Mass is our great prayer of praise.

Over to You

1. Take a few minutes to reflect quietly on your own and write down one or two of your deepest desires.

2. Do you agree with the statement that as soon as one desire is satisfied, we have another and then another? Explain with examples your point of view.

3. Can you explain the difference between the 'peace' that Jesus promises to us and the 'peace' that the world gives?

4. Describe an occasion when you have spent some time in prayer and how you felt afterwards.

5. Why is it important for us to go to Mass on Sundays?

Extension Work (2)

The Greatest Mystery of all Time

Do you like being a detective? Are you one of those who like solving mysteries? Delving into a mystery can be fascinating, it stretches your mind, it gets it working in lots of different ways. You are now going to start studying one of the greatest mysteries of all time. If you work hard, concentrate, think deeply, pray for the gift of faith and understanding, you are going to discover the greatest treasure on earth.

But remember, you must concentrate, it is not going to be easy. If you try very hard today, the lessons which follow will become easier, and soon you will be able to help others to discover this great mystery - the Mass.

"In the Mass we touch Eternity"

On the next page Bishop John Brewer shares some of his thoughts about the Mass. Some of the things he says you will already know and believe, others you may find difficult. This is where the journey into the Mass begins.

First of all read page 12 slowly and carefully. Then in your exercise book:

(a) Make a list of things he says which you already know and believe.

(b) Make a list of things you find difficult and will need help to understand.

In the Mass we Touch Eternity

"The Mass is our Catholic Faith in a nutshell. Every Mass is the whole Catholic Church celebrating the Death and Resurrection of Christ. It may have taken place physically nearly 2,000 years ago. But that's only because we live in time. God lives in eternity - in the ever-present, the ever-now. In the Mass we touch Eternity. What happened 2,000 years ago is made present in the Mass today.

"The past becomes the now. The Real Presence of Christ is real, not imaginary. The bread and wine are a mere disguise. Jesus Christ, the Son of God, becomes as present on the altar as when he was on the cross and turned to the good thief and said: "Today, you will be with me in Paradise." Do you recall when Jesus was dying on the cross and he bowed his head and said: "Father into your hands I commend my spirit"? He is present like that in the Mass.

"No other event in the history of this world can match the earth-shattering event of Calvary, when God died. No other event past, present or to come, can match the cosmic event that is taking place in your church today in the Mass. When Jesus died on Mount Calvary, the words came true: "Behold the Lamb of God, who takes away the sins of the world". Yes, the world was redeemed on Calvary once and for all, for all time. In the Mass, today's world is being redeemed. God smiles on the whole of humanity as a result of this Mass that you attend. For God the Father cannot resist the sight of His Son making the supreme sacrifice to redeem the whole human race. That is why we should have Masses offered for our special intentions. It is the greatest divine arm-twister that has ever been invented!" **Bishop John Brewer**

Section 2

The Opening and Penitential Rite
of the Mass

In this section you will

• understand the meaning of the sign of the Cross;

• reflect on God's love for us;

• know that we belong to God;

• know that at the beginning of Mass we are invited to 'call to mind our sins' and to ask for God's forgiveness.

We are often in need of Reconciliation

Words which Hurt

Sticks and stones may break my bones,
but words can also hurt me.
Sticks and stones break only skin,
while words are ghosts that haunt me.

Slant and curved the word-swords fall
to pierce and stick inside me.
Bats and bricks may ache through
bones, but words can mortify me.

Pain from words has left its scar
on mind and heart that's tender.
Cuts and bruises now have healed;
it's words that I remember.

Author unknown

Over to You

Think about this poem and then answer the following questions:

1. What happens when someone uses hurtful words to you?

2. What happens when you use hurtful words to others?

3. How do hurtful words separate us from God?

4. Read Matthew 18:23-35 'Parable of the unforgiving debtor'.
   What is the message Jesus has for us in this 'Parable'?

5. In which prayer do we find the same message?

Sin separates...
Forgiveness unites...

Extension Work
This is a true story. Read it very carefully.

A strange thing happened on Christmas Eve in 1937. A middle aged man, who worked as a labourer, went to visit an elderly lady at the house of a priest. He was very upset and tearfully begged the elderly woman to forgive him; she assured him that she already had. Before the story continues, you need to know these facts.

Maria Goretti, declared a Saint in 1950, died in 1902 at the age of 11, the victim of a young man's rage. When she resisted his advance, the man, Alesandro Serenelli, stabbed her over fourteen times. She died later in hospital, after saying of her murderer, "May God forgive him, because I have already forgiven him." The murderer, because he was still in his teens, was sentenced to thirty years in prison.

The middle-aged man was Alesandro Serenelli; the elderly woman was Assunta Goretti, Maria's mother. They later went to Midnight Mass together at a church containing a shrine to Maria Goretti.

Over to You

Alesandro could have waited until Mass was over before he met with Assunta.

1. Why do you think he did not do this?

2. Why do you think the Penitential rite happens early in the Mass?

The Sign of the Cross

At the beginning of Mass we make the sign of the cross. This is a sign that we belong to God - we are God's people. We belong to each other in God; not just in families. As God's people we call each other brother and sister.

When we make the sign of the cross we show that we belong to God and that we know that our life should be shaped by God's plan for us.

- When I touch my forehead I acknowledge that everything I think and say should come from God.

- When I touch my chest this indicates that my love is shaped by God's love for me.

- When I touch my shoulders I recognise that everything I do should be what God wants me to do.

God Loves Us

Can you imagine having someone

Who will always love you?

Who loves you as you are?

Who is always ready to forgive you no matter what you do?

Who knows you through and through?

Who even if you try to hide from him, he will search for you?

This someone is God.

We meet Jesus in the Mass

The greatest gift God has given to us is his only Son Jesus. In the Mass, Jesus comes to us in a very real way. In order to be worthy to receive Jesus, the first thing we do is to make the sign of the cross with the priest and to call to mind our sins and ask for God's forgiveness.

"To make the sign of the cross is to pray in the name and in honour of the Father, the Son and the Holy Spirit. God is outside our capacity to understand him. He is three persons: he is Father, he is Son and he is Holy Spirit. Each time we make the sign of the cross we are actually confessing that we believe that God is three and God is one."
Cardinal Basil Hume

Over to You

Read one of the following parables:

'The lost sheep' Luke 15:4-7

'The lost drachma' Luke 15:8-10

'The prodigal son' Luke 15:11-24

1. Why is there celebration in each story?

2. What does this tell us about Jesus?

We Belong to God

At Mass we receive life from God. When we were baptised we became members of God's family. We belong to God. In this relationship in God we are all brothers and sisters.

God teaches us how to live...

Therefore, to fail to live according to this teaching is to break relationships with both God and with one another.

Therefore, to seek and work for reconciliation, means turning to God from whom all good comes. Also we have to turn to one another and to admit our mistakes and our responsibility for them.

At the Beginning of Mass

We are brought together as the body of Jesus Christ. We are all members of the Church. So when we come into church for Mass we have a sense of being 'at home', of being where we belong in our Father's house.

At the beginning of Mass we try to remember all this.

In particular we are asked to examine the way we behave towards God and towards each other. Can we say that we have truly loved God and loved all the people with whom we have come in contact? Frequently we fail to live up to this great command of Jesus. So at the beginning of Mass we are invited to 'call to mind our sins' and ask for God's forgiveness.

With the priest we make the sign of the Cross to remind us that we are in the presence of God. He addresses us as 'brothers and sisters'. Then we are given a few moments to reflect on how we have treated one another and to ask for God's forgiveness for the times we have failed to be kind and thoughtful towards others.

Over to You

1. Work in pairs to compose and write out a 'Penitential Rite'.

2. Write a summary in your exercise book of what you have seen on the video.

The Penitential Rite

The celebrant invites the people to call their sins to mind, and to repent of them. He may then use the following:

Celebrant: Lord Jesus, you are mighty God and Prince of peace: Lord, have mercy.
People: **Lord, have mercy.**

C. Lord Jesus, you are Son of God and Son of Mary: Christ, have mercy.
P. **Christ, have mercy.**
C. Lord Jesus, you are Word made flesh and splendour of the Father: Lord, have mercy.
P. **Lord, have mercy.**

OR

C. Lord Jesus, you raise us to new life: Lord, have mercy.
P. **Lord, have mercy.**
C. Lord Jesus, you forgave us our sins: Christ, have mercy.
P. **Christ, have mercy.**
C. Lord Jesus, you feed us with your body and blood: Lord, have mercy.
P. **Lord, have mercy.**

OR

All: **I confess to almighty God; and to you, my brothers and sisters, that I have sinned through my own fault, in my thoughts and in my words, in what I have done, and in what I have failed to do; and I ask blessed Mary, ever virgin, all the angels and saints, and you, my brothers and sisters, to pray for me to the Lord our God.**

C. May almighty God have mercy on us, forgive us our sins, and bring us to everlasting life. Amen.

A True Story

This is a story about a Nun who lived in an American city. There, after many years teaching, she took up a job as a worker for the Diocese, helping people to understand justice and peace in their lives.

After some time of illness her doctor told her that she had cancer and needed chemotherapy, which involves chemicals being put into the body to destroy the cancer cells. Each week she went to the hospital for treatment. It worked well. She got better; the cancer was destroyed. On her last visit, when she was receiving her last infusion of chemicals, she looked around the waiting room at all the very sick people,

including some children. She felt fine and she thanked God that she had been cured. At 10.30 am she returned home. At 11.00 am the phone rang. It was the hospital.

They asked her to return immediately. She drove back there, puzzled. The hospital administrator and her medical consultant met her and took her into his office. They told her there had been a terrible mix-up. She had been given another person's mixture of chemicals. Slowly she asked if it was a serious mistake. Even more slowly they explained that it was, in fact, a fatal mistake. The mixture she had received would cause her death. There was nothing that could reverse it. She was stunned. Then she asked how long the process would take? When would she die? "In about six hours", they said.

She was devastated; she wept for quite some time. Gradually she became more composed. When they asked if there was anything she wanted, she began to speak. She asked first to see the nurse who had made the mistake. When he came he was in tears. She told him not to be too upset. "I've made many mistakes myself," she said. "It's easily done. Though none have had these consequences." Then she asked him to remember that it was, in some ways, providential that it had happened to her and not to someone else. "After all", she said, "as a religious Sister, I do not have a husband or children. It might have been much worse." She also said that her whole life was centred on Christ and that she was ready to go, through death, to meet him. This was what she had lived for.

Then she asked for a video camera to be brought. She spoke in front of the camera, making a film of messages for her community, her brothers, their children, her friends. She had no time to see them again. By this time it was 1.30 pm.

Then she asked for her religious superior to come, and the Archbishop. Everyone was in tears. She asked the Archbishop to celebrate Mass, there in the room. Together, with the doctor and the nurse, they prayed together, received Holy Communion and asked for the strength of God's grace.

By this time it was 3.00 pm and the Sister was beginning to feel weak and ill. She was taken to a private room and was put to bed. She went to sleep. At 4.00 pm she woke. Quietly she whispered her last wish to her Superior and to the Archbishop. She made both of them promise not to take any action against the nurse or against the hospital. She wanted them to take care against the same mistake happening again, but that was all. No blame; no compensation; no retribution. She was at peace, and ready.

At 6.00 pm she died.

Over to You

1. How do you think the nurse felt:
   (a) when he discovered he gave the wrong injection?
   (b) when the Sister forgave him?
   (c) that night when he was alone?

2. Have you ever had an experience of being loved and accepted after doing something that was wrong? Describe your experience.

3. What is the most important message in this true story?

Self-Assessment

Answer the following questions in your exercise book

In the lessons so far on the Mass:

1. What did you find most difficult?

2. What did you enjoy doing?

3. Did the time pass quickly? Why?

or

Did the time drag? Why?

4. Make a list of all the things you have learnt that you did not know before you started the topic.

5. Do you feel you have worked hard?
   (a) All the time?

   (b) Most of the time?

   (c) For a short time?

Section 3.
The Liturgy
of the
Word

In this section you will

• **know what is meant by the 'Liturgy of the Word';**

• **understand that God speaks to us here and now in the Scriptures;**

• **be able to listen to the Word of God and reflect on it.**

The Liturgy of the Word

The first part of the Mass is the Liturgy of the Word. The readings from the Old Testament, the Letters of the New Testament and from the Gospels. These are called the Word of God because the writers of the Bible were inspired by God. When these words are read at Mass, God is still active in them so that they come to us as a living Word.

The words we hear are not just a record of what happened long ago, stories from the past or messages that are hard to understand. They are a living word. In the next few lessons you are going to experience how they speak to us. God has a message for us today.

Scripture is the living Word of God

Over to You

1. Read the following passages very slowly and then choose the one you like most of all.

2. Stay with your chosen passage and read it over and over again.

3. Copy it into your exercise book and try to say why you chose it and how it helps or challenges you.

"Now if... God clothes the grass in the fields... how much more will he look after you?" (Luke 12:28)

"The Lord is my shepherd, there is nothing I shall want." (Psalm 23)

"Do not let your hearts be troubled, trust in God still, and trust in me." (John 14:1)

"If you ask for anything in my name, I will do it. If you love me you will keep my commandments." (John 14:14-15)

"In God alone there is rest for my soul." (Psalm 62)

"You are precious in my eyes." (Isaiah 43:4)

"If anyone loves me he will keep my word, and my Father will love him, and we shall come to him and make our home with him." (John 14:23)

"Your word is a lamp to my feet and a light to my path." (Psalm 119:105)

"Love your enemies, do good to those who hate you, bless those who curse you, pray for those who treat you badly." (Luke 6:27-28)

The Readings at Mass

Cardinal Hume and Bishop Nichols answer questions from pupils.

What does the WORD mean?

"We believe that the Bible is God's Word. The Bible is, as it were, God speaking to us. He has spoken to us all down the ages and for a long, long period up to when Jesus became man. So God became man, and then he was called the Word. 'The Word was made flesh' (John 1:14). So the Word is the word of God which we read in the scriptures. Jesus Christ is the Word of God in reality." **Cardinal Basil Hume**

Sometimes it is difficult to understand the readings at Mass; how can you help us?

"It always strikes me that it is important how we listen to these readings. We can listen to them as if they were stories about the past, for example, the story of the flood. Now it was a story about things that happened in the past. But we don't say this **was** the word of the Lord. We say this **is** the Word of the Lord. We believe that God is speaking to us through these words now. This **is** the Word of God. God is speaking to us now. We are trying to listen with our hearts because God is speaking." **Bishop Vincent Nichols**

But it is even harder to listen to some of the readings!

"Shall I tell you what I do when I am listening. I just try to hear one phrase, or one sentence, and I think, 'oh that's lovely, that's an attractive phrase.' I try to remember it, to hang on to it. It might be something that just speaks to me. It might be that if I am upset, it just gives me a bit of comfort. It might be because I am very happy and I think 'oh there it is'. Then I think God uses those words to get through to me, in a little phrase, in one sentence. So we try to listen to God speaking to us now in these words. And that is why I think we also say, 'This is the word of the Lord' now, for you and for me, each time we go to Mass." **Bishop Vincent Nichols**

Over to You

1. In your exercise book give examples from the passages of Scripture we have been reading:

(a) how God speaks to you;
(b) words which challenge you;
(c) words which comfort you.

Signs & Actions at Mass

Why do we stand when the Gospel is read?

"The four Gospels are the most precious part of the Bible. So when the priest comes to read it, we all stand up out of respect for this Word of God, which is the Gospel. And we do that in preparation to receive the Good News which Jesus both is and gives to us." **Bishop Vincent Nichols**

Why does the altar have candles?

"A candle gives light and a candle gives warmth. And when you were baptised (you were probably too little to hold a candle, and so your father probably held the candle) you were given a candle to remind you that because you were baptised you had to be like a little candle in the world. And if you think of the world as a very dark place, a little candle can make quite a lot of light. So even though we find the world a very big place, if you are a real, good follower of Christ, you can make a lot of difference. But a lot of people holding little candles, well they can make a big, big difference because they make a great big light and give out quite a lot of warmth.

If you go into a church on Holy Saturday night you will find there is a special service of the candles, and also we renew our baptismal promises. So candles have became very, very important in the life of the Church. I always like to think of myself as trying to be a little candle, to give light to people, to lighten up their world, and also to show them that Our Lord came to bring light." **Cardinal Basil Hume**

Why do we use incense at Mass?

"We use incense as a sign of the presence of God. The Gospel book is incensed. Incense is burned while the Gospel is being read, because God speaks to us in a particularly clear way." **Bishop Vincent Nichols**

Over to You

1. Draw a candle and write around it all the things it symbolises.

2. Choose one of the answers to the questions:
   (a) draw a picture to illustrate its meaning;
   (b) explain in your own words what it means.

The Word of God

Listening is often difficult. There is so much noise and so many distractions, so many words, some of which are not easy to understand. In order to understand what God is saying to us we need to listen not only with our ears, but also with our minds and hearts. God speaks to our hearts because God wants, above all, to speak to us of his love and care for us.

All of God's words to us are brought together in the person of Jesus Christ for he is the Word made flesh.

He spent his life responding to the needs and desires of all the people he met. He urged his followers to feed the hungry and give drink to the thirsty. But he did not want his disciples only to satisfy the physical needs of people; they were to meet their spiritual needs as well. When people came to Jesus hungry for food, he would give them something to eat, but he would also give them spiritual food. Here is the account from St. John's Gospel about how he did it.

The Gospel of St. John 6:5-14

Looking up, Jesus saw the crowds approaching and said to Philip, "Where can we buy some bread for these people to eat?" He only said this to test Philip; he himself knew exactly what he was going to do. Philip answered, "Two hundred denarii would only buy enough to give them a small piece each."

One of his disciples, Andrew, Simon Peter's brother, said, "There is a small boy here with five barley loaves and two fish; but what is that between so many?"

Jesus said to them, "Make the people sit down." There was plenty of grass there, and as many as five thousand men sat down. Then Jesus took the loaves, gave thanks, and gave them out to all who were sitting ready; he then did the same with the fish, giving out as much as was wanted.

When they had eaten enough he said to the disciples, "Pick up the pieces left over, so that nothing gets wasted".

So they picked them up, and filled twelve hampers with scraps left over from the meal of five barley loaves.

The people, seeing this sign that he had given, said, "This really is the prophet who is to come into the world".

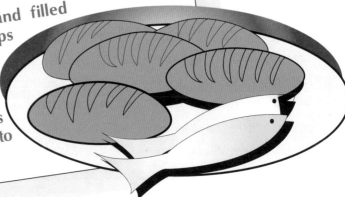

The Word of God

The day after the feeding of the five thousand, the crowd came looking for Jesus again. Jesus was concerned that they might be coming looking for more food or another miracle. He took this opportunity to speak to them of another kind of food.
He said:

"I am the living bread which had come down from heaven. Anyone who eats this bread will live for ever: and the bread that I shall give is my flesh, for the life of the world." [John 6:51]

When the people heard this, many of them found it too difficult to accept. They could not believe Jesus. Many of his followers turned away. Jesus turned to his Apostles and asked them:

"What about you, do you want to go away too?" Peter answered for all of them: "Lord, who shall we go to? You have the message of eternal life, and we believe; we know that you are the Holy One of God." [John 6:67-68]

The people were even more amazed than they had been the previous day. They began to argue, "How can this man give us his flesh to eat?" Jesus said to them:

"I tell you most solemnly, if you do not eat the flesh of the Son of Man and drink his blood, you will not have life in you.

Anyone who does eat my flesh and drink my blood has eternal life, and I shall raise him up on the last day. For my flesh is real food and my blood is real drink. He who eats my flesh and drinks my blood lives in me and I live in him." [John 6:53-56]

The Word of God

For Catholics the Bible is God's word. The Bible is, as it were, God speaking to us. He has spoken to us all down the ages until God became man in Christ. Christ himself is called the Word made flesh. So the Word which we read in the scripture is the Word of God, and Jesus Christ is the Word of God in reality.

When we listen to the Bible read in Church we are hearing God speaking directly to us. His Word is a living Word. If we listen carefully, God will speak directly to us.

Over to You

1. Slowly read again the words of Jesus in St. John's Gospel on the previous page and quietly think about them.

- **Think of the followers of Jesus.**

- **Think of the Apostles.**

2. If you had been there with them, which group do you think you would have been in? Give at least two reasons for your answer.

3. Imagine you are trying to help a new pupil who has come to a Catholic school for the first time. He/she has difficulty understanding the difference between our physical and spiritual needs. Try to explain the difference using this passage of scripture or another one that you know.

Homework

When you go to Mass on Sunday, listen not only with your ears, but also with your mind and heart to the Gospel. Take a piece of paper and a pencil with you.

1. Make a note of which Gospel it is.

2. Make a brief note of what it is saying to you.

3. When you get home, read the Gospel again and write a paragraph of what you believe God is saying to you in it.

Alternative Homework
St Luke's Gospel Chapter 6:27-38

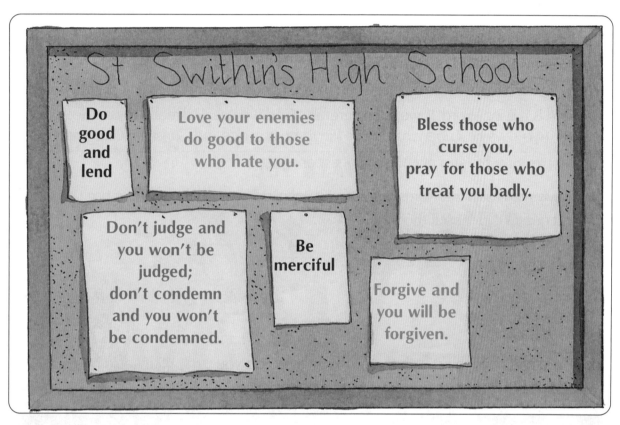

**Love your enemies
do good to those who hate you,
bless those who curse you, pray
for those who treat you badly.**

If you love those who love you,
what is special about that?
Everybody does that sort of thing.
If you favour those who favour you,
what is special about that?
Everybody does that sort of thing.
If you lend money to those you
hope will help you,
what is special about that?

Love your enemies;
do good and lend,
expecting nothing back.
Be merciful as God your Father
is merciful.

**Don't judge and you won't be
judged;
don't condemn and you won't be
condemned; forgive and you will
be forgiven;** give and you will be
given, a good measure pressed down,
shaken together, running over,
will be poured into your lap.

1. Read the passage on the previous page taken from St. Luke's Gospel.
   Think about it.

2. Draw up a plan to live as a very good Christian for two full days. Mention at least four things you could do.

3. After two days describe what it was like to be a very good Christian. Give practical examples of what you did. Write at least one page.

The Presentation and Offering of the Gifts

In this section you will

• **know what it means to offer gifts of bread and wine at Mass;**

• **know that at Mass we are united in the offering of Jesus himself to the Father;**

• **understand why there is a procession with gifts up to the altar.**

Offertory Gifts of Bread and Wine

We know Jesus used bread and wine at the Last Supper. That is why we use them. But there is also another meaning to them. The bread is like all the everyday things that we do, like getting up, going to school, going home, doing homework, doing the washing up, whatever. So the bread represents the everyday things. The wine is all the excitement and the joy, the special occasions, the parties, and the things that make us excited.

In the two symbols of bread and wine, it is as if we are bringing all the parts of our life and placing them on the altar. Jesus then takes them up as part of his offering. So we are offered to the Father with Jesus in his offering.

Over to You

1. Write a prayer for the Offertory.

• **Think first of what the bread represents for you.**

• **Then think of the wine and of what it includes.**

• **Use illustrations to help you.**

Offering Ourselves to God

In this part of the Mass we thank God for all his gifts to us: the gifts of life, of love, of friendship, of inventiveness and genius, his gifts of all good things. We recognise that God blesses us in so many ways. We come to Mass to offer our thanksgiving, our praise to God.

Why is there a procession up to the altar with the Gifts?

The Offertory starts with a procession when people bring us the bread and wine. Normally only two or three people bring up the Offertory gifts, but we should imagine that we are all walking up with them and offering ourselves with these gifts. The sign of our offering of ourselves is this bread and this wine. They are changed into the Body and Blood of Jesus and become an offering of Jesus himself. Together with himself Jesus offers all of us - our thanksgiving, our praise, our sorrow, to the Father.

Why is the water mixed with the wine?

The wine is going to be the blood of Jesus Christ, and the water is, as it were, us joining Him. The prayer that we say at that point explains this.

At this part of the Mass the priest says quietly:

"By the mystery of this water and wine we come to share in the divinity of Christ, who humbled himself to share in our humanity"

and

"Lord God, we ask you to receive us and be pleased with the sacrifice we offer you with humble and contrite hearts."

Offertory Gifts of Bread and Wine and Ourselves to God

The bread represents our daily routines, our daily effort, the ways in which we try to help others.

The wine represents the richness of our life: our laughter, our fun, our adventures, our hobbies, the good things we enjoy.

At the Offertory we can offer our whole life to Jesus. In that way he can unite us to himself and make us part of his offering of himself to the Father.

Over to You

1. Do a line drawing of Jesus offering himself to the Father.

2. Complete the picture by using a 'spider-type diagram' to make your offering, so that Jesus can unite it to his offering of himself to the Father.

Homework

Over the next two weeks you are asked to prepare a Mass Booklet which could be given to children to help them prepare for their First Holy Communion. You should now be able to explain to them:

(a) Penitential Rite.

(b) How God speaks to us in the Scripture Readings at Mass.

(c) Presentation and Offering of the Gifts. You should try to use your IT skills when possible. Spend 40 minutes on this homework tonight. Bring it to your next RE lesson so that your work can be checked by the teacher.

(d) Can you find a way of including in your picture the two prayers said silently by the priest?

Something beautiful for God...

The Gift we give to God,

God transforms into something beautiful.

Everything we give with a generous heart,

God accepts as though we had given everything.

Though what we have was first given to us by God.

Like the woman with a few dollars who went into the slums of a large city,

with no place to stay and no more money.

She gave to God her desire to tend the poor and dying.

God transformed her offering into hospitals and schools and places

for the dying,

into thousands of followers working across the globe.

Like the cup of water given to a little follower of Christ that is written into the eternal records.

Like the widow's offering given in God's Temple, greater than all the rest;

like the repentant woman's gift of perfume, offered with such love, and remembered for all time in the Gospel.

Like the boy's loaves and fishes transformed into a feast for the crowds.

Like the bread and wine we offer

to be transformed into the body and blood of Christ Jesus, The Lord.

Paul McHugh

Preparation for a class Mass

Group work

When you reach the end of this study it would be good to have a class Mass which you have helped prepare. You can start work on this now by planning a Mass booklet.

- Design a front cover for the booklet.

- Write out a Penitential Rite.

- Select two readings from the Bible, one of which must be from the Gospels.

- Select a Psalm to go after the first reading.

- Write out some bidding prayers, which should include a prayer for the Church, for the world, for the oppressed and suffering and for your local community.

- Select music and hymns and decide at which parts of the Mass they will come.

- Make plans to invite a priest to celebrate the Mass

Section 5.

The Eucharistic Prayer and Consecration

In this section you will

- know that at Mass we remember and we participate in Jesus' Last Supper and sacrifice;

- know that at the consecration, through the power of the Holy Spirit, the bread and wine become the body and blood of Jesus.

Eucharistic Prayer and Consecration

AT MASS, we remember and we participate in Jesus' Last Supper and sacrifice.

At the Last Supper which Jesus has with the apostles before he was crucified on the cross, Jesus gave them bread and said:

'This is My body'.

Then he gave them a cup of wine to drink and said:

'This is My blood'.

After that he said:

'Do this in memory of me'.

We believe the words of Jesus because we believe that he is God. He can bring about what he says.

At Mass the priest says these same words. He says them 'in the person of Jesus' - because he represents Jesus. So the bread and wine are changed into the body and blood of Jesus. We still see bread, we still see wine - but with our faith we say "This is Jesus' body, this is Jesus' blood".

From the very beginning after the resurrection of Jesus, the first Christians gathered to share that sacred meal in his memory. They call it the EUCHARIST, which come from a Greek word that means 'thank you' or to say thank you. The first Christians were firm in their faith that Jesus was present with them, just as truly as he had been in his physical body.

Saint Paul wrote to the first Christians at Corinth:

"This cup we use in the Lord's Supper and for which we give thanks to God: when we drink from it, we are sharing in the blood of Christ. And the bread we break: when we eat it, we are sharing in the body of Christ." (1 Cor 10:16)

At the heart of the Mass Jesus offers himself to his Father in a great act of love. We call this his sacrifice. We join Jesus in his offering of himself to the Father. He also offers us with himself to the Father.

Over to You

1. Explain in your own words what happened at the Last Supper.

2. Jesus tells his apostles to 'Do this in memory of me'. What does he want them to remember?

Extension Work

At Mass, we remember and we participate in Jesus' Last Supper and sacrifice

1. Read the account of the Last Supper, Luke 22:14-20.

2. Read the account of the Passover, Exodus 12:3-14.

3. What are the main differences between the Passover and the Last Supper?

4. Why is it important to make a link between the Passover and the Last Supper? Use the following explanation by Cardinal Hume to help you answer these questions.

"At Mass, we remember and participate in Jesus' Last Supper and sacrifice. It reminds us of the meal which Our Blessed Lord took when he celebrated the Passover, as it is called, at the Last Supper. It was a very special meal because they were celebrating something very important in their history, which is when the chosen people were liberated from Egypt. They were liberated from servitude and led into the promised land. That is what that meal was celebrating. At the Last Supper when Our Lord changed the bread into his body and changed the wine into his blood, he was also enabling us to bring Calvary and his death into our presence. Also he was bringing his resurrection into our presence." **Cardinal Basil Hume**

The Consecration

What does the Consecration mean?

At Mass, Jesus Christ becomes truly present to us in the bread and wine which is changed into his body and blood.

This is the heart of the tremendous mystery. This is the way in which God reaches out to us, to our day, to every place. He gives himself to us in the gift of Jesus the Son. Jesus of Nazareth was truly God and truly man, God the Son in our flesh and blood. Now, on the altar, the same Jesus, the same Son of God, becomes present in the sacrament.

How do we know this happens?

We know it only by faith. When he gave the bread to his disciples Jesus said: 'This is my body'. When he have them a cup of wine to drink he said: 'This is my blood'. Then he said 'Do this in memory of me'. He can bring about what he says.

At Mass the priest says these same words. He says them 'in the person of Jesus Christ'. They are as truly spoken at each Mass as they were at the Last Supper. What is said is brought about: the bread and wine cease to be bread and wine. They become the body and blood of Jesus Christ.

How is this miraculous change brought about?

This miraculous change is brought about through the power of the Holy Spirit. It was the Holy Spirit who, at the command - or word - of the Father, brought about creation. It was the same Spirit that raised Jesus from the dead. This same Spirit acts again in response to the words of Jesus as they are spoken by his Church, in the person of the priest.

Let us now link the Offertory with the Consecration.

This is the great mystery. The same Jesus who offered himself to the Father on the cross is present on the altar. We make our offering with the gifts of bread and wine. Through the power of the Holy Spirit the bread and wine become the body and blood of Jesus. Jesus makes that sacrifice of his body and blood present to us. He unites our offering with his to the Father.

Over to You

Make notes on how you are going to explain the 'Consecration at Mass' to the children preparing to make their First Holy Communion.

Section 6. The Sacrifice of Christ

In this section you will

• have some understanding of what sacrifice means in the Jewish and Christian faiths;

• know that Jesus became the perfect sacrifice so as to give all who believe in him eternal life;

• understand why Jesus is called the 'lamb of God'.

Prayer before the Cross

Lord Jesus Christ,

For love of us you embraced the wood of the Cross on Calvary. You laid down your life that we may be healed and forgiven of all our sins.

At baptism we were signed with the cross, and each day we bless ourselves with the sign of that cross.

Your Cross is the means by which you forgive us, heal us and save us.

May we be granted the grace to love your Cross and to always trust in the love it represents.

Help us to take up your cross daily in our lives so that we may be faithful to you in all things.

We make this prayer through the same Christ the Lord. Amen.

Sacrifice - Gift

Before we study the sacrifice of Jesus, let us first look at how sacrifice was understood in the Old Testament.

Throughout the ages, people have offered sacrifice to God. Sometimes their understanding of it was quite mistaken. Pagans used to sacrifice human beings. As God revealed himself (made himself known) to people they began to get a better understanding of what sacrifice involved.

In the Old Testament they used to offer sacrifice of animals, especially lambs, as a symbol of sorrow, repentance and love. In this chapter we are going to explore Abraham's experience. He believed God was asking him to sacrifice his own son, Isaac.

Sacrifice - Gift

In the Old Testament, sacrifice is mentioned in several places. One of the greatest events was when Abraham believed that God was asking him to sacrifice his only son Isaac.

The Sacrifice of Isaac

It happened some time later that God put Abraham to the test:
'Abraham, Abraham' he called. 'Here I am' he replied.

'Take your son,' God said 'your only child Isaac, who you love, and go to the land of Moriah. There you shall offer him as a burnt offering, on a mountain I will point out to you.'

Rising early next morning Abraham saddled his donkey and took with him two of his servants and his son Isaac. He chopped wood for the burnt offering and started on his journey to the place God had pointed out to him. On the third day Abraham looked up and saw the place in the distance.

Then Abraham said to his servants:
'Stay here with the donkey. The boy and I will go over there; we will worship and come back to you'.

Abraham took the wood for the burnt offering, loaded it on Isaac, and carried in his own hands the fire and the knife. Then the two of them set out together. Isaac spoke to his father Abraham. **'Father'** he said. **'Yes, my son'** he replied. **'Look,'** he said, **'here are the fire and the wood, but where is the lamb for the burnt offering?'** Abraham answered: **'My son, God himself will provide the lamb for the burnt offering'.** Then the two of them went on together.

When they arrived at the place God had pointed out to him, Abraham built an altar there, and arranged the wood. Then he bound his son Isaac and put him on the altar on top of the wood. Abraham stretched out his hand and seized the knife to kill his son.

'Now I know that you fear God'

But the angel of Yahweh called to him from heaven, **'Abraham, Abraham,'** he said. **'I am here,'** he replied. **'Do not raise your hand against the boy,'** the angel said. **'Do not harm him, for now I know you fear God. You have not refused me your son, your only son.'** Then looking up, Abraham saw a ram caught by its horns in a bush. Abraham took the ram and offered it as a burnt-offering in place of his son.
(Genesis 22:1-19)

Abraham & Isaac

Read Genesis 22:1-19

What were they thinking?

Abraham before and after the Angel spoke to him?

Sarah? (Isaac's Mother)

Isaac?

The two servants?

How do we interpret the story of Abraham and Isaac? (Genesis 22:1-19)

Abraham came to believe that God was asking him to offer his only child Isaac as a burnt offering to honour God. This idea corresponded to the practice in pagan countries where the worship of idols meant offering children in sacrifice. This savage ritual was later forbidden by Hebrew Law **(Leviticus 18:21)**.

Abraham believed that God had spoken to him. He was a man of great faith and in silence he obeyed. He entrusted his life and his future unconditionally to God. In fact, his faith was quite extraordinary. God had already promised him that his descendants would be as many as the stars of heaven. He wondered how could this happen if he sacrificed his only son but, nevertheless, he was prepared to do so.

As Christians we have the full revelation about God and know that he is a loving Father. That he should ask Abraham to sacrifice Isaac seems dreadful to us. That

Abraham, in his time could think as he did, however, is understandable.

What actually happened? Abraham carried out his intentions almost to the point of sacrificing his only son Isaac. THEN God intervened. Why? TO STOP HIM! A ram was provided for the sacrifice instead.

Because of Abraham's great faith in God he is remembered in the Eucharistic Prayer 1 of the Mass as 'our father in faith'.

"Father, look with favour on these offerings and accept them as once you accepted... the sacrifice of Abraham, our father in faith..."

Over to You

1. Imagine that you are either Abraham, Sarah or Isaac. Write an account of your experience.

2. Can you think of anyone today who has faith and trust in God like Abraham?

Abraham, Isaac and Jesus' Sacrifice

GOD GIVES his only Son to be the sacrifice. He fulfils the Old Testament Law of sacrificing lambs to God by offering the perfect sacrifice of his only Son, Jesus.

The ram caught in the bush was God's gift so that Abraham did not have to give up (sacrifice) his son to God. In the fullness of time, God gave up his only Son to be the sacrifice that takes away our sins. Instead of a ram for a son, Isaac, God now gives his own Son as the Lamb of God. This gift shows the great love God has for us.

The Lamb of God

AT COMMUNION in the Mass we say with the priest:

"Lamb of God, you take away the sins of the world: Have mercy on us."

"Lamb of God, you take away the sins of the world: Have mercy on us."

"Lamb of God, you take away the sins of the world: Grant us peace."

For the early Israelites, who kept flocks of sheep and goats, a lamb brought to mind something pure, innocent - as good a gift as possible to offer God.

- **Jesus is 'the pure and innocent one', without spot or stain of sin.**

- **He is 'the gift God gives to us' (he is truly God).**

- **He is 'the gift God accepts from us' (he is truly man).**

- **Jesus is the 'Lamb of God'. He is the perfect, absolute gift.**

If we are to be included in this sacrifice, then we have to be identified with him. We have to be one with him. We have to be part of this sacrifice that makes things right. We do that by our baptism. We are united in Jesus by taking part in the Mass and receiving his body and blood in Holy Communion. We become part of that peace, the bond, which is sharing in the kingdom of God.

"This is the Lamb of God who takes away the sins of the world..."

Over to You

1. Think of the sacrifice of Jesus at Calvary alongside Abraham's sacrifice.

2. In the sacrifice of Jesus, who represents:
   (a) Isaac?
   (b) the Ram?
   (c) Abraham?

3. The picture below shows a lamb holding a cross. What do you think this picture is meant to symbolise?

4. Do you, or your parents know any pub called the 'Lamb and Flag'? Find out where the name comes from.

Sacrifice and self-surrender

The English word 'sacrifice' comes from a Latin word meaning 'to make sacred' or 'to make holy'. We think of sacrifice as making an offering to God. Sacrifice is about choosing to think about others before yourself. It is about doing something for someone else, or spending time with others and not expecting anything in return. It can also mean giving up something of value.

Over to You

1. Think about a mother and father. What sacrifices do they make for their children?

2. What does a sports person sacrifice in order to excel at sport?

3. What does a musician sacrifice? For whom?

4. Can you think of others who make sacrifices?

5. What do you sacrifice for others?

During his life, Jesus shared many meals with sinners and tax-collectors. When he was asked why he did this, he replied: "It is not the healthy who need the doctor but the sick... I did not come to call good people but sinners." (Matthew 9:12-13) Jesus was showing compassion and reaching out to those who needed him. He lived for the lost, for sinners. At the Last Supper, he showed how this LOVE would reach its full meaning:

"This is my body given for you...
This is my Blood shed for you...
Do this in memory of me".

With these words, Jesus embraced his death upon the cross. He would experience being abandoned by his friends, mocked and made fun of, and cruelly put to death.

"...but now he showed how perfect his love was." (John 13:1)

Jesus sacrificed himself in love, Jesus offered his life for his friends. Jesus gave his life in self-surrender to God.

Over to You

Write a story of self-surrender. It can be about a mother and child, or about someone sacrificing themselves for someone else. Show how the person sacrificed himself/herself.

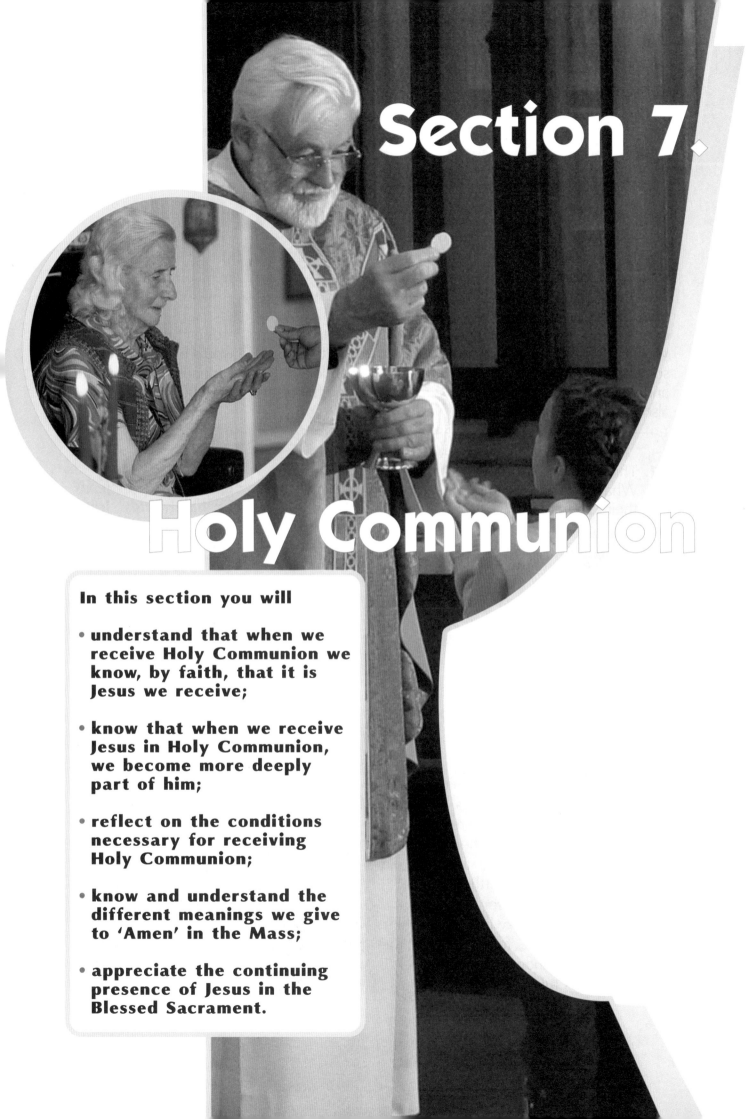

Section 7.

Holy Communion

In this section you will

- **understand that when we receive Holy Communion we know, by faith, that it is Jesus we receive;**

- **know that when we receive Jesus in Holy Communion, we become more deeply part of him;**

- **reflect on the conditions necessary for receiving Holy Communion;**

- **know and understand the different meanings we give to 'Amen' in the Mass;**

- **appreciate the continuing presence of Jesus in the Blessed Sacrament.**

The Bread of Life

Read John 6:1-15; 51-58 (Pages 28-29)

Read the passages very carefully and enter into the scene which is taking place. Remember you already did this when you were studying the 'Word of God'.

Task A

Imagine you were with Jesus when the events were taking place. The following day you are stopped by a journalist who is not a follower of Jesus and knows very little about him. However, she has heard that strange things have been happening and wants to get an article for her newspaper. Think carefully before you answer her questions.

Journalist:

1. Excuse me, were you present on the hillside yesterday?

2. Did you hear the sermon of the prophet from Nazareth?

3. Can you explain what happened there?

4. What do you think he was trying to say?

5. Do you consider yourself one of his followers?

6. Do you think he will get his large following back? Why?

Task B

Work in small groups to produce the newspaper article. Remember that more than one person's opinion can be stated. Use your IT skills to present it in a way which will catch the reader's eye.

Holy Communion

We share fully in the sacrifice of Christ by receiving the body and blood of Christ in Holy Communion. When we receive the host it is not bread we receive: it is the body of Christ present in the form of bread. When we receive from the chalice, it is not wine we drink: it is the blood of Christ present in the form of wine. When we receive Christ in Holy Communion, we become more deeply part of him, and so are given a promise of sharing his life fully in heaven.

When we receive Holy Communion we know, by faith, that it is Christ we receive. We welcome him into our hearts. The time after Holy Communion, then, is a time of most special prayer. During it we speak personally to Jesus who is present within us. We speak our words of thanks, of love and of longing. We speak to him as a most dear friend who has come to us. We speak to him as God, our Lord, and our Master.

When we receive Holy Communion we show what we believe by the way we behave. It is Christ our Lord who comes to us. We are full of respect, reverence and love. This sacrament is the greatest gift God has given to us, the Church. So we treasure this gift in every way.

It is helpful to remember that even the Apostles did not understand Christ's words about eating his flesh and drinking his blood. Not until the Last Supper did they see what he meant and they did not really understand until after the Resurrection.

Over to You

1. What does our faith tell us:

   (a) When we receive the host at Mass what is it?

   (b) When we receive the chalice at Mass, what do we drink?

   (c) Why is the time after Holy Communion very precious?

   (d) What should we do after Holy Communion?

   (e) What is the most important gift we could receive?

2. Work in pairs and think of how you are going to explain 'Holy Communion' to pupils getting ready to make their First Holy Communion. Make notes which will help you to complete this section of your homework.

3. At home, complete this section of the booklet on Holy Communion.

Extension Work

A friend who is not a Catholic has asked you to explain what you understand by Holy Communion. Write out a full explanation for him/her.

Amen

The meaning of 'Amen'

"There is another lovely time when we say Amen in the Mass. When you receive Holy Communion, the priest says 'The body of Christ' or 'The blood of Christ' and you say 'Amen' which is the same as saying 'Yes, I do believe'. This is the body of Christ, this is the blood of Christ. Amen, so be it. As well as expressing faith, you are also saying 'Yes, I do need Our Lord. I am a disciple of Our Lord. So you say 'Yes' 'Amen'. I need this body and the blood of the Lord if I am going to live my life of faith as best I can.

And you are also saying another thing in that 'Amen': You are saying 'Yes, I do see myself as part of the Church because it is the priest who offers you Holy Communion. In the Eucharistic Prayer the Bishop and the Pope have been mentioned, so when we say 'Amen' we are saying Amen to them as well.

'Amen' is saying 'Yes, I am a disciple of the Lord'. 'Amen' is saying 'Yes this is the body and the blood of the Lord'. 'Amen' is saying 'Yes, I accept the ministry of the priest and the bishop. I am a member of this Church'. 'Amen' is a small word, but it is a very powerful word, because it is you saying, 'Yes, I am in all of this - this is me too.'" **Bishop Nichols**

Over to You

1. When we receive Holy Communion what are the three meanings we give to 'Amen'?

2. Watch the section of the video on Holy Communion. What does Cardinal Hume say about 'Amen'?

3. Research into when 'Amen' is said in other parts of the Mass. Explain in your own words what you are saying 'Amen' to in those parts of the Mass.

Receiving Holy Communion

When we receive Holy Communion we approach the altar in procession. We go up together, as the People of God. To join in the procession is to express our faith. It is to say 'I am a member of this People of God. I am a member of the Church'.

To be a member of the Church and to be ready to receive Holy Communion involves certain things.

We can receive Holy Communion if we are baptised Catholics and have gone through a period of preparation to make our First Holy Communion. If we have committed a grave sin we must go to confession before we receive Holy Communion.

In order to be a full member of the Catholic Church we must be united with our Bishop and with the Pope. It is also essential to believe in the teaching of the Catholic Church as expressed in the Creed.

What happens if a person is not a full member of the Catholic Church?

Many people join in the procession, even if they are not able to receive Holy Communion. They join in the procession because they share much of the faith of the Catholic Church. To walk together is to express a shared faith. But when they reach the priest or the eucharistic minister

they seek a blessing. Some are too young to receive Holy Communion. Some are not 'in full communion' with the Church and so do not receive Holy Communion.

Over to You

Going up to receive Holy Communion is to walk in a procession. It is not waiting in a queue.

1. How should I behave?

2. What should I be doing?

3. What do I think about in a queue?

4. What should I think about in this procession?

5. Can you describe some people who join in the procession but do not receive Holy Communion. Explain the reasons why they do so?

The Blessed Sacrament

Jesus has promised to be with his Church 'until the end of time' (Mt 28:20). One of the ways in which he fulfils this promise is though his abiding (permanent) presence in the Blessed Sacrament.

The Blessed Sacrament is what we call the consecrated hosts which are kept in the tabernacle so that we can always pray in the presence of Jesus. The Blessed Sacrament can also be taken to people who are very ill and unable to get to Mass.

Why did Jesus choose to remain present with us?

When Jesus died on the cross he knew that he was doing the will of his Father. This means that Jesus knew that his Father wanted, more than anything else, to let people know how much he loved them. Jesus' death on the cross is the message of God's love for all people. Jesus continues to give us that same message, by his abiding presence in the Blessed Sacrament. His message is: God loves you. I am the presence of God's love for you, always here.

It is God's way of showing how much he loves us.

Jesus is present as our food and drink.

He is also giving us another message by his presence in the Blessed Sacrament: the most important thing in life is to do the will of God, to do what our loving Father wants

us to do. Jesus said that to do the will of the Father was 'his food and drink'. Now he is present to us as our food and drink, in order to teach us always to keep in our minds the will of the Father.

This continuing presence of Jesus in the Blessed Sacrament is very special to all Catholic churches. This presence makes them an abiding (permanent) place of prayer and contemplation. This presence is what makes our churches a place of consolation and wonder.

Pope John Paul II teaches us...

The sanctuary light tell us that Jesus is present In the tabernacle. We genuflect as a sign of respect.

'The Church and the world have a great need for Eucharistic worship. Jesus awaits us in the sacrament of love. Let us not refuse the time to go to meet him in adoration, in contemplation full of the faith, and open to making amends for the serious offences and crimes of the world. Let our adoration never cease.' (John Paul II, Dominicae cenai, Cf Catechism 1380)

The Blessed Sacrament is kept in the tabernacle, but when we have Benediction it is placed on the altar in a monstrance. Benediction is a special time of prayer, adoring Jesus in the Blessed Sacrament.

The Blessed Sacrament

Over to You

In your own words explain:

1. What the Blessed Sacrament is.

2. Why we have it in our Church.

3. List, or draw the ways in which the abiding presence of Jesus in the Blessed Sacrament is seen in our Churches, or in your school chapel.

4. Write a prayer that you will say next time you visit a church and pray before Jesus present in the Blessed Sacrament.

5. Read the following passage.

   Our understanding of this abiding presence tell us that it is one of the ways in which Christ continues to give himself to us, out of love. It is the same gift that he gave when he offered his life on the cross. We believe that the presence of Christ in the Eucharist begins at the moment of the consecration. It endures as long as the outward forms of the bread and the wine last. Therefore, Catholics always offer adoration to the sacrament of the Eucharist, not only during Mass, but also outside of it, reserving the consecrated hosts with the utmost care in the tabernacle. The Blessed Sacrament becomes a focus of our prayer, especially during Benediction. (Cf. Catechism 1377, 1378)

6. Design a notice for outside the chapel or church door explaining to people about Christ's abiding presence. The information in this passage is to guide you.

Section 8.

Our Mission

In this section you will

- know and understand why you should go to Mass on Sundays;

- know and understand that at the end of the Mass we are sent out to be witnesses of Jesus in our world;

- know that Holy Communion is the food which gives us the life and strength to do Jesus' work in the world.

"Go in peace to love and serve the Lord."

One way to live out the challenge of the Mass...

Young people are bored when they don't understand something or don't know what to do. Being bored at Mass springs from forgetting that we go to Mass to pray.

We don't go to Mass to be entertained. We go to Mass to participate in the death and resurrection of Christ, and so share in his new life. Hence Sunday is the day for going to Mass, above other days. We have to be very alert during the Mass so that we can fully participate in what is happening.

Over to You

1. It is part of your mission to help other pupils in the school understand what you now know about the Mass. Work in pairs to go over the most important points of the Mass:

   - Penitential Rite
   - Liturgy of the Word
   - The Presentation and Offering of the Gifts
   - The Eucharistic Prayer and Consecration
   - The Sacrifice of Jesus
   - Holy Communion.

2. On your own make a poster explaining what happens at each part of the Mass and what you have to do during it.

   - This should involve writing as well as drawing.
   - Explain what the people present should do.
   - Use computer skills where possible.

Extension work

Find out the names of the martyrs who died because they refused to give up the Mass, e.g. Edmund Arrowsmith, John Southworth.

Our Mission

When we receive Jesus in Holy Communion we are made more deeply part of the Church, which is his body. Holy Communion is our food giving life and strength. This food is Christ and it gives us his life and his strength, so that we may live as he wants us to live, and to do his work in our world. By receiving Jesus in Holy Communion we are enabled to bring his presence into the world: our home, school, playground, football pitch, in fact, wherever we go. We become his co-workers.

Part of our 'mission' is to go to Mass. We have a very important duty to go to Mass. Going to Mass is a public act. By going to Mass we give public witness to our faith in the Catholic Church.

At the end of the Mass we are sent out to be Christ's witnesses in our world. We have been nourished by God's Word and by Christ's body and blood. Now we are ready for our mission.

St. Teresa of Avila reminds us in her writings:

'Christ has no body now on earth but yours. Yours are the only hands with which he can do his work... Yours are the only eyes through which his compassion can shine upon a troubled world. Christ has no body now on earth but yours.'

Over to You

On a small sheet of paper illustrate how we can be Christ's presence and carry on his work in a specific place. For example, by visiting the sick, helping the homeless, helping an old person, befriending a lonely pupil.

(a) In groups draw up a list of places and activities where we could carry on Christ's work.

(b) Each person chooses a different one and develops it in words or by a drawing. Illustrate how Christ wants us to live and do his work in our world.

(c) The pieces of paper are then put together to form a large poster to illustrate how the Mass gives us strength and courage to live as Christ wants us to live and do his work in our world.

Glossary of Terms

Altar: A table for sacrifice.

Amen: It is saying 'I do believe' See page 54.

Baptism: The sacrament in which, by water and the word of God, a person is cleansed of all sin and reborn and made holy in Jesus to everlasting life.

Benediction: It is a special time of prayer, adoring Jesus in the Blessed Sacrament.

Blessed Sacrament: The real presence of Jesus in the form of consecrated bread.

Celebrant: The priest or bishop who leads the liturgy.

Chalice: The cup for the wine at Mass.

Communion: We receive the body and blood of Jesus.

Consecration: The action of the priest at Mass which, by the power of the Holy Spirit, changes the bread and wine into the body and blood of Christ with the words "This is my body"; "This is my blood".

Creed: We profess our belief in the basic truths of our faith.

Diocese: A geographical area which contains many parish churches under the care of a bishop.

Eucharist: Literally 'Thanksgiving'. It is sometimes used for the Mass, or the body and blood of Jesus in particular.

Eucharistic Prayer: A prayer, praising God, calling down the Holy Spirit, retelling the Last Supper story, and with the words of Jesus changing the bread into his body and the wine into his blood.

Forgiveness: Saying sorry/accepting that someone is sorry.

Genuflect: To go down on one knee in the presence of the Blessed Sacrament when you enter or leave a Catholic church.

Gloria: A song of rejoicing in the goodness of God. This is said or sung.

Gospel: An account of Jesus' life or teaching.

Glossary of Terms

Host: The piece of bread that is used in the Mass, to become the body of the Lord Jesus.

Humble: Modest, not looking for notice.

Last Supper: The meal, associated with the Passover, which Jesus celebrated with his disciples in the upper room the night before he died.

Liturgy: The worship of God in public prayer. The Liturgy of the Church is made up of ceremonies for which there are clear and fixed guidelines.

Liturgy of the Word: Readings from the Old and New Testament.

Mass: Also called Eucharist. The celebration of the death and resurrection of Jesus.

Miracle/Miraculous: An extraordinary event attributed to supernatural power.

Monstrance: A vessel in which the Blessed Sacrament is placed for adoration.

Offertory: That part of the Mass in which the unconsecrated bread and wine are offered to God.

Penitential Rite: It is a form of words we use when we ask for forgiveness and healing for any sin that separates us from each other and from God, and in which we receive God's forgiveness.

Responsorial Psalm: It is a hymn of praise and is often used as our response to God speaking to us.

Rite: The formal set of words and actions to be used in a Liturgy.

Sacrifice: The word comes from a Latin work 'to make sacred' or 'to make holy'. It is the highest form of adoration in which the priest, in the name of the people, makes present again Christ's offering of himself to the Father. In doing so, we acknowledging that he is Lord and Saviour and that we are totally dependent on him.

Sanctuary light: A small lamp, usually red, placed near the tabernacle.

Glossary of Terms

Scripture: The writings in the Bible.

Self-surrender: To hand oneself over.

Sign of the Cross: Catholics begin all prayers by calling on the name of God. We call on the name of each person of the Trinity and sign ourselves with the cross which has become the symbol of our salvation.

Symbol: A symbol is an object, word, or sign that points to, or almost makes present, a deeper truth. A religious symbol is something that represents some sacred truth or mystery of the faith.

Tabernacle: A special, decorated container, or safe, in which the Blessed Sacrament is reserved. It is to be found in a prominent place in the church.

Vestments: Clothes to show that the priest, when celebrating Mass, takes on the new identity of Jesus.

Worship: Reverence and respect paid to God.